MARK

W9-AHZ-555

LONG BEACH PUBLIC LIBRARY
101 PACIFIC AVENUE
LONG BEACH, CA 90822

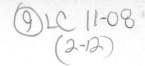
⑨LC 11-08
(2-12)

Rainbows
of the Sea

For Lisa and Jeremy

The sculptures in this book were built from paper. The artist colored the paper using paints and then added texture by scoring, pleating, and embossing. To make the final shapes, she cut and sometimes folded the painted, textured forms and glued them together.

Before making the sculptures for this book, the artist carefully observed the living things of the sea. She also studied photographs in books, and drew each shape from many different angles.

The sculptures were photographed using special lighting and focusing to bring out the vibrant colors and give the impression of being underwater.

Copyright © 1998 by Meredith Thomas

All rights reserved.
No part of this publication may be reproduced, except in the case of quotation for articles or reviews, or stored in any retrieval system, or transmitted in any form or by any means, electronic, mechanical, photocopying, recording, or otherwise, without written permission from the publisher.

For information contact:
MONDO Publishing
One Plaza Road
Greenvale, New York 11548
Visit our web site at http://www.mondopub.com

Printed in Hong Kong
98 99 00 01 02 03 04   HC   9 8 7 6 5 4 3 2 1
98 99 00 01 02 03 04   PB   9 8 7 6 5 4 3 2 1

Editorial management by Sally Moss, White Kite Productions Pty Ltd
Paper sculptures photographed by Adrian Lander
Designed and typeset by Sandra Nobes, Tou-Can Design Pty Ltd
Production by The Kids at Our House

Library of Congress Cataloging-in-Publication Data
Thomas, Meredith.
    Rainbows of the sea / by Meredith Thomas.
        p.   cm.
    Summary: Uses their colors to introduce a variety of sea animals, including sky-blue soldier crabs, cobalt-patterned angelfish, and blue-black manta rays.
    ISBN 1-57255-431-2 (pbk. : alk. paper). — ISBN 1-57255-432-0 (hc : alk. paper)
    1. Marine animals—Color—Juvenile literature.   [1. Marine animals. 2. Color.]   I. Title.
    QL122.2.T455   1998
    591.77—dc21   97-45723
                                                            CIP
                                                            AC

3 3090 00850 8428

Rainbows of the Sea

Meredith Thomas

photography by
Adrian Lander

MONDO

Rosy dawn glows on a pale silk sea.
Sun rises now, what can you see?

Tiny sky-blue soldier crabs
tread lightly over sands.

Cobalt-patterned angelfish
flit through coral hands.

Massive blue-black manta rays
sweep across the deep.

Purple-legged lobsters
huddle in a heap.

Dainty rose anemones
stretch their stinging wands.

Fighting flame-red fiddler crabs
clash by mangrove ponds.

Honey-orange sea dragons
race past kelpy dells.

Buttery little lemonfish
drift beneath the swells.

Hungry green-gold pipefish
search in seagrass waves.

Graceful jade-flecked turtles
glide through cool blue caves.

Soaring rainbow sailfish
shimmer, leap, and shine . . .

Flick their mighty tail fins
and vanish in the brine.

Sun sinks low and light is fading.
Brilliant hues give way to shading.

Moon path skips on ocean's gray.
Bold colors await the bright new day.